Seek Peace
& Pursue It

Women, Faith, and Family Care

Elizabeth Soto Albrecht

Faith & Life Resources

A division of Mennonite Publishing Network
Mennonite Church USA and
Mennonite Church Canada

Scottdale, Pennsylvania
Waterloo, Ontario

Seek Peace & Pursue It
Women, Faith, and Family Care
Copyright © 2010 by Faith & Life Resources, a division of Mennonite Publishing
Network, Scottdale, Pa. 15683, and Waterloo, Ont. N2L 6H7

Unless otherwise noted, Scripture text is quoted, with permission, from the New
Revised Standard Version, © 1989, Division of Christian Education of the National
Council of Churches of Christ in the United States of America.

Hymns referenced in this book are from *Hymnal: A Worship Book* (Faith & Life
Resources, 1992), *Sing the Journey* (Faith & Life Resources, 2005), and *Sing the Story*
(Faith & Life Resources, 2007).

All rights reserved. This publication may not be reproduced, stored in a retrieval
system, or transmitted in whole or in part, in any form, by any means, electronic,
mechanical, photocopying, recording or otherwise without prior permission of the
copyright owners.

The content for this book was sponsored jointly by Mennonite Women USA and
Mennonite Women Canada.

International Standard Book Number: 978-0-8361-9520-0.
Design by Merrill Miller, Mary Meyer
Cover photo: DesignPics.com/Ron Nickel, composite
Printed in the USA

16 15 14 13 12 11 10   10 9 8 7 6 5 4 3 2 1

To order or request information, please call 1-800-245-7894 in the U.S.
or 1-800-631-6535 in Canada.
www.mpn.net

Contents

Foreword

My friend, Elizabeth Soto Albrecht, is a courageous woman to tackle the subject of peace in the family. Living out our ethical and biblical commitment to peace as Anabaptists is at best difficult, but doing it within the context of family goes to the core of our commitment. That is where it is hardest. I appreciate Elizabeth's use of the word *Shalom*, which includes mind, soul, body, and our relationship with God, others, and creation. This is a broader understanding of what peace is all about. You will find depth and breadth to this study.

Raising three children and finding my understanding of peace at odds with my relationship with family has been a journey. At times the journey has been joyful, and at other times painful. To talk about peace in the family is difficult. We have been socialized to think that family matters are private. Therefore, those who have been victimized within their own families are left voiceless.

Elizabeth challenges us to see Scripture through the lens of being a woman, and to understand how the ethical and biblical teaching of peace must start with our families. Women and men are created in the image of God. They can choose to relate to each other in unhealthy ways that are the consequence of sin, or choose to live out God's intended vision for men and women. This understanding alone can greatly influence how we live out our peace/*Shalom* commitment.

In this study, Elizabeth puts scholarship and practice together. It is not a study for the fainthearted. It is a study for those who are serious about learning what it means to be a woman of God and a family (in the broadest sense) committed to peacemaking. The examples of Jesus speak not just about confronting violence, but of just relationships that prevent violence and shape who we are as individuals, families, and communities of faith.

May you experience God's grace as you engage in this study.

Iris DeLeon Hartshorn
Portland, Oregon

Preface

here is a saying in my country, "*Es mejor prevenir que tener que lamentar*" ("It is better to prevent than to lament"). The older women in our family gave us many pieces of good advice, and this is one of them. I believe in preventive and healthy measures for our minds, bodies, and souls. Why not for our families?

The goal of this Bible study is to motivate church women to examine our family life and create steps to become families of God, where God's peace is present. We need to "seek peace and pursue it" (Psalm 34:14b) if we really want to have healthier families—not only eating well, but living in peace and well-being with each other.

I am a convert to Anabaptism, having received my second baptism three decades ago in a small Mennonite church in my home country of Puerto Rico. I am enchanted with Jesus' message of peace. I am a pacifist at heart, and my desire is to inspire Mennonite women to carry out God's message of peace—starting in our homes. I know we sometimes have trouble putting Jesus' teachings into action. My prayer is that as women come together to study the Word and pray, the Holy Spirit will show us the way.

This Bible study contains practical ideas for sowing the seed of true peace, while examining everyday actions. The questions at the end of each lesson guide women in being accountable to each other in the changes we need to make in our families and in our hearts. When I use the word *family* in this book, I am mostly referring to the family of origin (for singles) and the immediate family/nuclear family (for those with children and/or spouse).

I have written so much on family violence that I embraced this opportunity to be positive in building peaceful families of God. I write as a practitioner and also as a parent that struggles with making the right decisions. Remember, the only person you can change is yourself; that change is a starter for a family system to start shifting. Focus on what you need to do and let God do the rest. We cannot choose our birth families, but we can choose how we want to live our lives.

When we sit around the table to talk about God and our humanity we create a community of kin—people that belong to the same family. **You will notice that in these sessions the word kin-dom replaces kingdom.** Kin-dom refers to the reign of God. It describes not what is, but what the church is to be. The word highlights the difference between Jesus' kin-dom and the kingdom of this world. Jesus invited everyone into the same relationship with him; all are kin in God's family.

I encourage you to memorize individually or as a group Colossians 3:12-17, which presents the most beautiful message of peace for our families. Allow this text to guide your relationships in a Christ-centered, peaceful way.

In a serving spirit,

Elizabeth Soto Albrecht
Lancaster, Pennsylvania

A Word on the Use of This Guide

Spiritual growth involves learning to know God through the Scriptures and through life experience. Thus the sessions in this guide begin with a scriptural overview and move to personal experience through the visuals and thoughts of the gathering time. The "Deepening" part of each session returns to reflection on Scripture, and is followed by integrating questions that relate the lesson to our own lives. The closing brings together both scriptural insights and life-lessons in an atmosphere of prayer.

Women can use this guide in a variety of ways.

1. Both individual reflection and/or group sharing. An individual can study the Bible text and meditate on the words, perhaps using a journal to make entries and notice how God is walking with her. Or a group of friends may sit around the kitchen table and study the lessons together.

A single woman can use these lessons as a time to reflect on her biological family and friends, to pray for them and claim healthier ways of relating.

2. A more traditional approach. If the sessions are used in a more formal Bible study, be sure to include within your circle single women, single mothers, widows, divorced, and married, making the group intenionally diverse. Embrace all of these women's experiences—the voices of different ages, occupations, and cultures or ethnicities. We have much to learn from each other, and God uses many ways to "speak truth" in our lives.

3. Shorter meditations. The group or individual might want to use only the overview, visuals, and gathering for shorter meditations. A more elderly group, for example, may not be inclined to ask the deeper, probing questions. They might be very responsive, however, to sharing stories and memories sparked by the section on gathering.

Whatever the makeup of your group, pray for spiritual growth in an atmosphere of trust, confidentiality, and respect. As women of faith, may we grow in confidence and wisdom as we receive our gifts from God and share them with others.

one . . . .

Becoming Families of Peace

READING: Psalm 1

OVERVIEW

The Psalms are prayers and songs full of real human feeling and life experience. Psalm 1 begins with the beautiful image of a "tree planted beside streams of waters." Read the psalm in a contemplative way, meditating on the image of a tree. What type of tree does your life resemble? In what soil have your roots grown? If you have experienced uprooting because of death of a loved one, separation or divorce, emotional and physical distance from a sibling or your biological family, how has that affected you?

VISUAL: Tablecloth, tree seedling or branch, glass bowl or pitcher of water

GATHERING

Alicia and Teresa met at church and developed their friendship in the women's fellowship. They decided to meet for prayer and coffee twice a month. Teresa had been part of the church most of her life and became Alice's spiritual mentor. As they met one morning, Teresa asked, "How is your family doing?" In a sad voice Alice responded, "I am still making ends meet. I'm still looking for a job. As a family we haven't had so much stress since the kids' dad left."

Alice and Teresa's conversation about this difficult time opened the door to talk about choices Teresa could make toward peace in her family. Ask yourself: Is God's peace in my family? If not, what has happened and how is that affecting me? These are hard questions, but we must ask them in order to move toward a healthier and more peaceful family.

DEEPENING

Psalm 1 sets the standard for a life of obedience to God's laws. It presents two kinds of people—the wicked and the righteous, represented by the fruits they yield. Consequences follow our choices and actions.

We find the seeds of transformation inside of us when we are willing to go to the roots of problems and face our fears.

Throughout history, our human tendency has been to choose the easy path instead of the more challenging one. But Jesus, too, made history, choosing to do God's will even though it meant suffering. True discipleship means following Christ. It is an individual choice, but a family choice as well. We find the seeds of transformation inside of us when we are willing to go to the roots of problems and face our fears. The strength to work at change comes from our hearts. Romans 12:2a says, "Do not be conformed to this world, but be transformed by the renewing of your minds."

There are many subtle and seductive ways to take a wrong turn, but we are given a second and third chance with Christ.

We can choose life and begin building a family of peace. Peace is much more than just the absence of conflict, sickness, or calamity. *Shalom* means a state of physical, mental, and social well-being, both alone and with other human beings and God. As Christians, we aim to be peacemakers living out the values of the *kin-dom** of God, best illustrated in Jesus' life and teachings.

In the Bible, we read of many different types of families:
- Families with no children—Sarah and Abraham, Hannah and Elkanah
- Extended families—Peter's family included his wife's mother
- Females as heads of households—Rahab, Lydia, widows
- Siblings living together as adults—Lazarus, Mary, and Martha
- Immigrant families—Joseph's family, Naomi and Elimelech
- Created families—Naomi and Ruth
- Intercultural marriages—Boaz and Ruth
- Adoptive families—Mordecai and Esther, Pharaoh's daughter and Moses

These families, like our own, experienced love and envy, conflict and harmony, sickness, struggles, and happy times. Like them, we can rely on God for help as we seek to follow kin-dom ways.

INTEGRATING

1. What biblical family in the above list is most like your family? What kin-dom values did this family demonstrate?

2. What individual and family practices help you become more like a tree "planted by streams of waters"?

....
* See Preface, p. 8

3. Read "The Seven Manifestations of a Healthy and Peaceful Family" on pages 65-66. Reflect on this list and consider your family's current well-being. Pray for each member of your family.

CLOSING

Sing together: "Make me a channel of your peace," #56 in *Sing the Journey*.

Pray: *God of Peace, you call us to be peacemakers. Daily remind us of that calling and help us to create families of peace, despite the obstacles we may face. Let us start with choosing peace for ourselves. Amen.*

two · · · · · · · · · · · · · · ·

Family Unity Through Forgiveness

READING: Genesis 45:1-15

OVERVIEW

Genesis 45 tells of Joseph's reunion with the brothers who sold him into slavery. Chapters 37 to 47 relate Joseph's story, emphasizing the older brothers' envy for Joseph because they saw how "their father loved him more" (37:4). These negative feelings accumulated, ending in his brothers trying to eliminate him. Because Reuben intervened, they did not kill Joseph, but dropped him in the pit of a dry well and then sold him to merchant traders on their way to Egypt.

In Genesis 45, Joseph's love for his brothers won out over bitterness and resentment, and he was able to embrace them. He had evidently worked through his feelings during his time in Egypt, and was eager to help his family in their need.

VISUAL: Tablecloth, vining plant

GATHERING

Each month at my church, we recognize those celebrating birthdays, anniversaries, or special events, and pray for them.

One Sunday a couple stood up and announced they were celebrating their 47th wedding anniversary that day. Interrupting our happy applause, the wife quickly said, "I have become aware that part of our success in marriage has been both of us learning the art of forgiveness." Those words are full of profound truth. In order to have unity, we need to learn how to *forgive*.

How is it that we drift apart from the people we love? We are reminded of the fragility of relationships when we hear of yet another divorce or children taken away from their parents because of abuse or neglect. We cannot take for granted the gift of family, but must work for unity within it. At family reunions, we are grateful for how each generation has contributed to our history. Yet we realize that serious differences

Conflict is a normal human reaction, because we are social beings. But using violence is not a normal way of resolving these differences in the family.

can produce conflict among the family members. Conflict is a normal human reaction, because we are social beings. But using violence is not a normal way of resolving these differences in the family. We must learn to live with different opinions or ways of doing things, and forgive when conflicts arise.

DEEPENING

Christians have sometimes misinterpreted being a *pacifist* as being *passive*. The first is related to action; the second is associated with tranquility. To be a peacemaker means to work for peace, to do justice in the midst of oppression. The kin-dom value here is *Shalom*—the Hebrew term for peace, well-being, and health. At times of broken relationships, Jesus calls us to act in peaceful ways: do no evil, do not retaliate. To practice this is not easy. We feel it it is humiliating and even hurtful to ourselves.

But if the goal is to have unity in the family, whether extended, biological, adopted, or perceived, we must work at this intentionally. We do not reach unity by avoiding others, but by working for peaceful resolutions. Living in harmony with others and loving those who have hurt us is a spiritual skill.

The story of Joseph calls us to revisit the concept of forgiveness. This is an especially hard issue when a woman has been sexually violated or assaulted, or has experienced a spouse's infidelity. No one can prescribe forgiveness; it must be born within the heart of the one offended, sometimes in response to a process of repentance by the offender. At other times, it is a letting-go of the offense.

Holding on to resentment can cause hatred, which in turn is a leading cause of violence. The clue for transformation is not to allow resentment to make a bed in our hearts and minds. Can we live in peace, even when a sibling or parent or relative has hurt us? Joseph had all the reasons to be resentful toward his brothers, but he decided to be led by love instead of hate. He held his brothers accountable for their actions, but he forgave them.

Forgiveness is a long journey, a path less traveled. It can be painful and difficult, but God promises to be with us with every step.

INTEGRATING

1. List on chart paper or a board areas where we need forgiveness in the family.

2 . How can we find reconciliation in those instances? When do we need to "let go" in order to forgive?

3 . What did Joseph do in order to forgive?

4 . How did Joseph's brothers suffer the consequences of their actions?

5 . In what ways does a vining plant remind us of a family?

CLOSING

Sing together: "Bind us together, Lord," or
"Put peace into each other's hands," #87 in *Sing the Journey*.

Pray:
Parent God, may we be one,
As you and Jesus and the Holy Spirit are one.
Cement our unity in your Word,
Confirm our togetherness by your presence,
Reassure us through the love of Jesus, our Savior. Amen.

three . . . .

Parenting with Love

READING: Ephesians 4:26-27; 6:1-4

OVERVIEW

Paul's letter to the Ephesians gives good advice for both parents and children. His core message is clear: "Be imitators of God, as beloved children, and live in love, as Christ loved us" (Ephesians 5:1-2). He urges readers to live life as it should be lived by God's people, preserving unity.

Ephesians 6:1-4 first addresses children, those with the least power. Then it directly asks parents not to abuse their social and religious power in raising their children. Paul may be questioning the old belief, "These children are my property; I can do with them as I please." In the new community of faith, children should not be treated as objects, but as human beings, a gift from God to be cared for. We can use the advice from Ephesians 4:26-27 in the context of parenting and managing anger. We need to recognize that we need help to do this.

In the Anabaptist tradition, the body of believers helps to raise each child in the faith. It takes a village to raise a Christian believer and to help parent children with love.

VISUAL: Tablecloth with framed family portrait or photo of a child

GATHERING

The famous saying, "It takes a village to raise a child" is true for the church, too, as all are involved in caring for the children of the congregation. My African American neighbor, Darlene Byrd (block captain of our street), once shared, "I consider all the children that live on my block *my* children. I want to know who they are, and who they live with, in order to be community." Whatever our relationships with children, as adults we feel some degree of responsibility to care for "these little ones." That means we need to learn, on a community, family, and individual level, how to parent with love.

DEEPENING

As parents, we struggle with the fear of doing things wrong and wanting to do them right. Parenting skills are learned—unfortunately, children do not come with batteries included or a manual to follow. We tend to repeat the parenting of our mothers and/or fathers, whether healthy or unhealthy. We learn new ways by seeing others use certain techniques or skills and incorporating them into our parenting role. Today, many organizations, including churches and schools, offer creative ways to parent teens, toddlers, infants, school-age children, and young adults.

As a community of faith, we collaborate in the never-ending task of raising children. We must learn to detect if those parenting skills are based on love or fear, on controlling the other or on true peace-building.

First Corinthians 13:13 speaks of "faith, hope, and love, but the greatest of these is love." The number one value of the kindom of God is to love and to treat the kin as of equal value to yourself. That love is shown in the practice of self-control.

Notice that Galatians 5:22-23 begins the list of fruits of the Spirit with love and ends it with self-control. Exercising self-control in the name of Christ's *Agape*-love keeps us from being controlled by anger. Practice the affirmation phase, "I control my anger; anger does not control me."

The past leaves imprints on our lives, influencing our parenting. Some imprints are full of warm fuzzy memories; others are too painful to remember.

The past leaves imprints on our lives, influencing our parenting. Some imprints are full of warm fuzzy memories; others are too painful to remember. If we claim healing in the negative imprints, it is not enough to say, "I will never commit the same mistake." We need to admit the influence of those imprints and confess our shortcomings as a single parent or parent couple, an aunt with no children, or an adult who doesn't like being around children. And we must commit ourselves to learning new and better skills of parenting with God's love.

The first step toward change is simply admitting we need help and recognizing our lack of love in dealing with children. The need and desire for change is the energy builder that will help us look for help. There are plenty of resources available; all we need to do is to start looking. Ask your church to start a Sunday school class on parenting. Engage the adults in your household to attend together. Be sure to agree together how to reinforce the new rules of love in the home.

Love is tough. The clue for success in parenting is "being consistent." Do not give up. Parenting with God's love promises to bear the fruits of justice and peace.

INTEGRATING

1. How do we parent through a child's lifespan? What are the challenges in parenting young children? Teens? Adult children?

2. How is parenting our own children different from parenting our grandchildren?

3. How do multi-generational families living in the same home parent with love? How can spouses who have very different parenting styles parent together?

4. How can parents involve children in decision making, but still take their role as parents?

5. How can the church be the "village" for families with children?

6. Check out the STEP program (Systematic Training for Effective Parenting), www.steppublishers.org. This curriculum encourages parents to use positive, nonviolent strategies such as active listening, giving choices, and providing logical consequences to behavior.

CLOSING

Sing together: "Put peace into each other's hands," #87 in *Sing the Journey*.

Pray: *Loving God, help us to be loving to the children in our lives, as you are loving to us. Give us wisdom and courage to love as you love. Amen.*

four . . . .

Nurturing for Peace

READING: Psalm 34:1-14; James 1:19-25

OVERVIEW

Psalm 34 speaks of deliverance from trouble as coming from God but pursued by the believer. Verses 11-14 acknowledge that a change in direction is possible even in the midst of trouble. This psalm gives us hope when we feel powerless against evil. It tells us that God has set us free to both seek and achieve peace.

In the same spirit, James moves us to be doers of the Word and not just hearers. He urges us to be consistent in listening and acting in accordance with God's Word. The image of a mirror reminds us that our behavior sometimes does not reflect God's *Shalom* in a broken world. In a loving way, James is reminding his readers, "Don't forget who you are." We need to keep in mind that we are made in the image of God. Forgetting who we are compromises God's kin-dom.

VISUAL: Tablecloth, several small stand-up and hand-held mirrors

GATHERING

How do we nurture peace in our family in a culture that accepts verbal violence and disrespect? Examine this exchange between a teenager and his mother:

"Mom, everyone in my class uses curse words!" he says, upset that she has once again called attention to his use of profanity.

"In our Christian family we have values," she replies. "It's not acceptable for you to curse. You are using God's name in vain, putting others down, and not living up to our Christian values."

Is it possible to raise our children to value the Christian way of peace? As a parent, I choose to believe that, even if the task isn't easy, we are called to bear witness to the Prince of Peace. Yet peace must start in the intimacy of our homes, forming a family with God's values and not the values that the world influences us to follow.

DEEPENING

Becoming doers of the Word highlights God's righteousness, God's quality of "making things right." The kin-dom of God brings about right relationships, new behavior based on the values of justice and peace, moving us from wrongdoing to "right doing." The best way to nurture a culture of peace is by making things right. In living out kin-dom values, we bring to life the Word of God, nurturing others for peace.

As adults set in families, we need to nurture our spirituality: our connection with God. In other words, we must make sure our beings are centered in God, so that we can mirror God's values for all members of the family, from youngest to oldest. James clearly states that it is not just *talking* about the Word or being religious but *doing* the Word that makes God's justice shine in the midst of so much injustice. We care not only for our immediate family, but for all of God's family, nurturing peaceful relationships.

The kin-dom of God brings about right relationships, new behavior based on the values of justice and peace, moving us from wrongdoing to "right doing."

This commitment requires first an intentional personal nurturing of peace within our own mind, body, and soul. Then we are able to work creatively at nurturing that peace in our relationships with those who are dear to us. This peace then radiates out to our neighborhoods and larger communities. Repeat an affirming statement each day during the next week: "Today I will seek peace and pursue it for my spirit and my family's well-being," or "I will nurture peace today."

INTEGRATING

1. Give an example from your life when you have not nurtured peace. Reverse the situation and share how it could have been different.

2. Give an example of a time when you've said you're sorry to your children for something you have done.

3. Give an example of a reflection your children or others in your family have caught from your "mirror."

4. What Christian values do you want to pass on to the next generation?

CLOSING

Sing together: "Make me a channel of your peace," #56 in *Sing the Journey*.

Read the sending words from *Sing the Journey*, #158.

Pray: Merciful God, *help us to forgive ourselves for the times we have failed to be loving to others in our families. Give us strength to ask for forgiveness, and help us to show your love in the future. Amen.*

five . . . .

Power in the Family

READING: Matthew 20:20-28

OVERVIEW

As women, we intercede in prayer many times for our own children, our nieces and nephews, or friends' children. Surely we want the best for the children near to our hearts. In this story from Matthew, we do not hear the voice of the two disciples. We can only suspect that they desire the recognition their mother is requesting for them. The same story is found in Mark 10:35-45, except that it is the disciples who approach Jesus directly.

The disciples have seen God's power manifested through Jesus in his teaching and healing acts. Later in the Gospel, they are promised that they too will be doing this and much more. So what are these two disciples lacking that induces them to make such a request? In the book of Revelation, we are told that the lamb of God—God's son Jesus—is the one sitting on the right-hand side of God. Jesus is right that he doesn't have the power to change something his father had already determined. Jesus, as an excellent master, takes the teachable moment and focuses the theme on "serving one another," offering a new dimension of power.

VISUAL: Tablecloth, serving tray with plate of food, napkin, and glass of water

GATHERING

Sometimes, as women, it is easy for us to get caught up in our own busyness and our own perceived need to serve others. If I find myself falling into such thinking, I remember a poor family who wished to invite us over for a meal when we lived in Bogota, Colombia. We objected, "Oh, no, let us host you!" Their insistence on serving us opened our eyes in a new way. Another woman shared a similar story in which the other person told her, "Please, let us serve you—don't rob us of our blessing." It is important to allow others to be blessed by letting them serve us as women, just as we are blessed by serving others.

DEEPENING

In the Bible text, Jesus makes an interesting connection between serving and his disciples' struggle for positions of power. The topic of power can be uncomfortable, especially for women. We tend not to claim the power we have. Or we have painful experiences with power being used against us in abusive relationships. As parents, we are responsible by law to represent the interests of our minor children. We are given that power and are held accountable if we misuse that power through abuse or neglect.

As women, we need to recognize that experiences with power are often defined by sex, color, and class. Not all women have the same power. As a woman of color, I am very much aware of those disparities. Can you remember a time when your eyes were opened to the realities of power imbalance because of sex, color, or class?

In God's kin-dom there is equal space for all at the table of the Lord. We are all valued equally. In our Christian lives and in churches we try to live up to this principle, but sometimes fall short. We are called to live out the values of God's kin-dom, but the earthly attitudes of sexism, racism, and classism force themselves in. As women, we have been hurt by these views, yet we still must believe in equality. Jesus strongly confronted these attitudes during his ministry.

We confess as Christian women that we can be driven by serving. We lose ourselves in serving others— our families, the needy . . . Sometimes we may be called to just *be*.

"The Son of Man came not to be served but to serve" (Matthew 20:28a) is Jesus' clear and final statement regarding the disciples' request. What a simple message for such a big problem! We are called in God's kin-dom to serve.

This message is not new for women, because of our traditional role. We now not only serve at the kitchen table and in the church fellowship hall, but in serving communion and in preaching. We confess as Christian women that we can be driven by serving. We lose ourselves in serving others—our families, the needy. I have learned in my part-time job as a chaplain that I am not called to fix others' problems, but to walk with those in pain. To accompany those that are hurting, even our own sisters, means to recognize our helplessness to take away the pain. That is hard for mothers, because we see our children crying and want to make it better. Sometimes it is possible, but at other times we may be called to just *be*.

To *be* is a spiritual exercise. It means to listen carefully, to ask what the other really wants, and not impose our desire to "fix it." Perhaps it is to go beyond just bringing in a casserole for the family that is grieving and to be Jesus' presence, allowing healing tears to flow.

INTEGRATING

1. What is power? When we choose to serve, what happens to our power?

2. In what ways can we receive gracefully from those with less power—the poor, children, etc.?

3. How do we deal with the tension between simply being present and trying to make things better?

4. One definition for power is "the energy to produce change." Think about family members who have influenced you and produced change in your life. What types of actions or attitudes had the most power to influence you?

CLOSING

Sing together: "Will you let me be your servant?" #307 in *Hymnal: A Worship Book.*

Pray: *Caring God, we want to serve others. Give us strength to overcome the temptation to do too much. Give us the power to simply* **be** *with others. Help us to demonstrate the values of your kin-dom. Amen.*

Created in God's Image

READING: Genesis 1:26-31; 3:14-19

OVERVIEW

The story of creation is found in two fascinating narratives, written and preserved within the ancient tradition of male centeredness. We honor and respect these accounts, but remember that they are products of their time. Traditionally, the Christian church has read the creation story in Genesis 2:4–3:24, which emphasizes a hierarchical understanding of creation, focusing on Adam/man being created first and Eve/woman created last.

We will focus on the first creation account from Genesis 1:1–2:4a. The NRSV version of the Bible reads, "God created humankind in his image . . ." (Genesis 1:27). Here humanity (*ha-adam*) is made up of two beings, male and female. Their relationship is equal rather than hierarchical. Both reflect the image of God, not found in the rest of creation. In this account, God creates both genders at the same time and partners with them, giving them the task of administering creation. In God's declaration of making humanity "in our image, according to our likeness" (1:26), there is a sense of companionship with humanity. Creating the two beings at the same time shows their equality and need for mutual companionship.

VISUAL: Tablecloth, picture or sculpture of a man and woman, apple

GATHERING

A young woman friend recently shared how she was told in her home, "You can be anything you want to be." At home, she never experienced limitations because of her sex. When she began working out in the world, she started to feel the stereotyping and limitations employers place on women, and had the same experience at church. Yet she believed inside herself that "we are all created in God's image."

The first place we experience the difference between women and men is in the family. In the beginning, we assume this difference is normal. We can even go through life's different stages never questioning these roles—reproducing them and reinforcing them in our newly established families.

This session takes us back to the beginning of gender—to Genesis, the creation of woman and man. In doing this, we can recover God's intention of making men and women of equal value. The question we need to struggle with is: Why have Christians placed so much importance on the details of of creation, justifying male power over women, humankind over the rest of creation?

DEEPENING

In the garden, the first man and woman lived in harmony with all creation and with God. In Genesis 3:14-19, we read about the breaking of that harmony because of human disobedience. Three consequences for that disobedience have ruptured God's intended order: enmity between humans and nature, the domination of man over woman, and the subjection of humanity to endless labor in the land. In verse 14, the word "woman" represents humankind, and the serpent embodies nature. Verse 16 describes the power struggle of man over woman, and her pain in bearing children. Her labor points to how maternity will define her role in society and subject her life to a man. Verse 17 declares that man's hard work will never satisfy him. He will be subject to the demands of working the land, and enslaved to the work he himself has created.

The three "curses" are natural consequences of humans' actions. They represent a violent breaking of the *Shalom*/harmony that God intended us to enjoy.

These three "curses" are natural consequences of humans' actions. They represent a violent breaking of the *Shalom*/harmony that God intended us to enjoy. Through Jesus' teachings, we can restore the harmony that was broken. We can choose better ways for women and men to relate to each other. Bearing children will no longer control a woman's life, or labor on the land a man's life. There is a different path—the way of nonviolence illustrated by Jesus.

We are created in God's image! How wonderful can that be? Claim this blessing for your life today. Dismantle the "curse" and live up to the *Shalom*/salvation God has given you through Jesus Christ. You are a woman of God, made in God's image and redeemed by God's son Jesus.

INTEGRATING

1. In what ways do you see God's image in women? In men?

2. How do we embrace God's redeemed image of women and men through Jesus?

3. What did you learn from your parents about what it means to be a woman?

4 . How does the division of tasks/toys we give to boys and girls influence children's understanding of gender?

5 . The image of God is still active in us. How do you perceive God's image in your life? How do we partner with God to bring back *Shalom*?

CLOSING

Sing together: "New earth, heavens new," #299 in *Hymnal: A Worship Book.*

Pray: *Creator God, help us to remember that as women we, too, are made in your image. Help us to live our lives accordingly. Amen.*

The Strength of Being a Woman

READING: Ruth 1:15-22

OVERVIEW

Ruth is the story of a widow who returns to Bethlehem with her widowed daughter-in-law. The women are displaced, with no man to protect them, but they react with resourcefulness. As my pastor once said in a sermon, "These are two women walking single file," returning to Bethlehem with no spouses, with empty wombs and empty-handed.

When Ruth resisted the suggestion that she return to her people and her land, she declared her loyalty to Naomi. What type of mother-in-law was this who inspired Ruth to make such a profound commitment? The women had only each other and an uncertain future in Bethlehem. The word "Bethlehem" in Hebrew means "house of bread." Perhaps Naomi knew only that she was walking away from famine and going toward food. In a man's world, the women knew they would need to work hard, even in "the house of bread." How did Ruth and Naomi learn to overcome their limitations? What strength did they gain from facing calamities together?

VISUAL: Tablecloth, several friendship bracelets, lighted candle

GATHERING

Teresa shares with Alicia, "You have been a gift for me from God." Tears of gratitude roll down her cheeks as she adds, "I admire the way you make your spiritual growth with Christ a priority." Alicia responds in a humble voice, "I should be the one thanking *you* for being my prayer friend and a role model for my life." Teresa and Alicia are affirming each other's strength as women, a strength directed at supporting the other and not criticizing.

We are born female and male, but we become feminine and masculine as we are socialized. We learn to behave in a "masculine way" and a "feminine way." Depending on the families into which we are born and the culture, girls' lives may be restricted to domestic roles and boys' roles outside the home. Although times are changing, and there are fewer limitations for girls, there is still an expectation that girls learn to clean the house and cook. Mothers have the power to raise their children free from sexist rules; change must start at home to impact society. Think of times you weren't permitted or given the opportunity to do things your brother or male cousins did, and felt it was unfair. If you come from an egalitarian home, share how different it was from your neighbors'.

We celebrate the strength women have, both physically and emotionally. But we need to recognize that a patriarchal society does place a value difference between genders.

What are your strengths? If you are studying with a small group, go around the circle and name a strength you have seen in each woman. Write the strengths others have seen in you on an index card and place it in your Bible. Read the list when you feel down and remember that God and others value you.

DEEPENING

Living in a technical age with access to computers, email, Facebook, and Twitter, we may think people aren't hurting for communication. But how many of these tools lack the face-to-face contact we all need? People feel lonely even when married. Fear of being alone and fear of closeness are two extremes we find in people who depend on connecting with others through a cell phone, iPod, or Blackberry.

Human beings are relational creatures, made in the image of God. We need community and to live in communion with each other. The New Testament calls this *koinonia*, an integral part of the emerging churches in the book of Acts. *Koinonia* requires sharing both materially and spiritually. It means companionship among believers and union with the

Just as Ruth joined in the suffering of Naomi, *koinonia* allows us to make that human connection with those who are hurting.

Holy Spirit. Just as Ruth joined in the suffering of Naomi, *koinonia* allows us to make that human connection with those who are hurting. Without the element of *koinonia* we cannot build the kin-dom of God. We need to come together in one spirit, as in one body, to live out the Word.

How ironic that Ruth, a non-Israelite woman, played a key part in the ancestry of King David and later Jesus, the Messiah (Matthew 1:5-6). Because of her commitment and loyalty, Ruth was redeemed in history. Jesus' teachings demonstrated the upside-down kin-dom, in which "the smallest of these will be the greatest." There is no small act in God's eyes and Ruth, in her stubborn clinging to Naomi, a woman who could not give her a future, was redeemed. We can name many strengths of Ruth, but the greatest was her commitment to

Naomi's God, when she declared, "your God will be my God." Ruth saw in Naomi's faith a God that was different from the ones she knew in Moab.

One of women's many strengths is valuing the company of other women as we walk this journey of faith together.

INTEGRATING

1 . What strengths did you see in your mother or another significant female in your life? How was she able to share her gifts?

2 . List examples of gifts women use in the home, church, and workplace. How do we support one another even when our gifts and calling are different?

3 . What strengths do you see in yourself that can bring peace in your family?

4 . Reflect on the role of female friendships and mentoring relationships in your spiritual journey. How can other women help us identify and use our gifts?

CLOSING

Sing together: "Take, O take me as I am," #81 in *Sing the Journey.*

Pray: *God of all humanity, help us to recognize our beauty and our gifts, and the gifts of other women. Give us the courage to use our gifts for your service, wherever that might be. Amen.*

eight . . . .

The Strength of Being a Man

Reading: Ruth 3–4

OVERVIEW

In this story, it seems at first that Boaz is responding to Ruth's actions. But he knows that the widow Naomi has just returned to town, accompanied by a younger woman. He notices Ruth gleaning in his field and has compassion for her situation. He orders the other women to leave plenty of grain behind for Ruth to pick up.

One possible meaning for the name Boaz is "in him is strength." In Ruth 2:11, when Boaz speaks to Ruth for the first time, how does he express his strength as a man? It matters to him that Ruth is supporting Naomi, and he rewards her for it. As kin to Naomi's husband, Boaz is represented as a "redeemer." Although he is not a close relative, he finds a clever way to help the two widows. The story presents Boaz as one who does more than is expected of him. The two defenseless women need not only the seed of grain, but the seed of children. Boaz is aware of his power and uses it to help. Ruth is redeemed, saved from a widow's life and a childless life.

VISUAL: Tablecloth, photo of man with family or children, symbols of strength (hammer, rock, etc.)

GATHERING

A woman nearing retirement shared in a women's circle her story of raising boys and coming out of an abusive spouse relationship. She said, "I was 30 and a mother of four sons, with my oldest approaching puberty. I realized that if I didn't change and openly value the gifts of masculinity, I would harm my own sons." She smiled as she told this story to our group, ending it by saying, "Recently I shared this long-ago decision with my son and daughter-in-law. My daughter-in-law thanked me."

In this lesson we examine Boaz's actions in helping Naomi and Ruth. You might wonder, if this is a serious Bible study for women, why we are talking about men and their strength. We cannot honestly talk about women's lives without mentioning how men influence us. When we speak about family relationships we need to include all of its members: sons and daughters, fathers and mothers.

The questions we ask are: How sensitive can men be to women's reality? Can men be tenderhearted without losing their masculinity? There are healthy ways to express masculinity that do not involve force, sexism, or violence. Men and women need each other in order to live out the full image of God.

DEEPENING

In order to build God's kin-dom on earth, we need harmony and solidarity among women and men. Solidarity means walking in the shoes of another person, to walk beside the person that needs our help. Boaz understood that Ruth needed help. She could depend on his strength and tenderheartedness to walk with her through this hard time. In our antagonistic society, we need each other to challenge imposed oppression.

Men, too, feel frustrated when they are expected to be the sole breadwinner. Today we have fathers willing to stay home with little ones and mothers earning income for the family. Men who choose the role of stay-at-home father feel at times belittled, even by their extended families. Solidarity means standing beside those men that have chosen to live out the change.

As women, we cannot make these changes for men, but we can educate boys and youth to be aware of cultural pressure and to resist.

Transformation must come from both women and men. As women, we cannot make these changes for men, but we can educate boys and youth to be aware of cultural pressure and to resist. Transformation can begin by saying and believing:

- Yes, boys and men can cry!
- Any type of violence toward women and men is unacceptable.
- Being affectionate does not require the use of sex.
- To be strong means to be sensitive.
- Men belong to the home, too.

INTEGRATING

1. How can we parent our sons and other young men in our churches to be strong and peaceful men?

2. What is the difference between wanting to be rescued by men and valuing the strength of men?

3. Think about unhealthy expressions of maleness you have experienced or witnessed.

4 . Invite women to affirm the gifts they see in the men and boys in their lives.

5 . How do we see the gifts of Boaz in men today?

CLOSING

Sing together: "Like a mother who has borne us," #91 in *Sing the Journey*.

Pray: *God of love, give us wisdom as we nurture the men and boys in our lives. Help us to encourage in them the gifts of gentle and sensitive caring for others. Amen.*

nine . . . .

Roots of Violence in the Family

READING: 2 Samuel 10 and 13

OVERVIEW

In the Bible we find horrible stories of violence, including accounts of women being killed, abused, or raped. We ask, why were these stories preserved?

In 2 Samuel 10, we read of King David's abuse of a woman he desires. From his rooftop, he sees Bathsheba taking a private ritual bath and invades her house. Bathsheba is just a subject in David's kingdom. As a woman under the power of the king, can she say no? Later, the prophet Nathan confronts David, comparing Bathsheba with a lamb that was stolen. David has sinned in God's eyes.

Three chapters later, we find one of David's sons committing sexual violence. Family systems theory would be quick to highlight patterns of behavior in David's family. The sin repeats itself. Chapter 13 tells of the beauty of Amnon's sister, and that he "fell in love with her" (13:1). But what does Amnon's final action disclose? Sexual abuse is about control and power, not about love. In the end, Tamar's brother Absalom kills Amnon.

VISUAL: Tablecloth, photo of a family torn in two

GATHERING

A pastor gently approaches a woman who has attended church with her family for a few years. He has noticed her crying on several occasions after worship. She does not participate in the women's group and is usually silent. Today she has come to church without her husband. "How is it going?" the pastor asks. The woman cannot speak, but tears fill her eyes. The pastor asks again, this time in a pastoral care manner: "If your tears had words, what would they tell me?" The woman responds in a low voice, "I am hurting . . ."

In looking at ways to help family life be healthier, we need to look at reasons families are unhealthy. Reports on domestic violence in North America inform us that one in three women will be impacted by violence during her lifetime. The state of Pennsylvania in 2005 registered 180 deaths resulting from domestic violence. If home is a safe place, why do the majority of assaults happen in the home of the victim, by the hand of a person she/he knows?

Destructive Power and Control

• Using coercion and threats (to leave, commit suicide, to hurt another)

• Using intimidation (to make afraid through looks or actions, smashing things, hurting pets)

• Using emotional abuse (to put another down, name calling, making someone feel crazy or guilty, playing mind games)

• Using isolation (to control another's actions or location, who the other relates with or reads; using jealousy to justify isolating another)

• Minimizing, denying, and blaming (making light of or denying controlling behavior, not taking another's concerns seriously, saying the other caused the controlling behavior)

• Using children (as intermediaries, threatening to take the children, inducing guilt about the children)

• Using gender privilege (to treat another like a servant, make all the decisions, being the only one to define gender roles)

• Using economic abuse (by preventing another from getting or keeping a job, taking money, withholding money or information about money)

• Physical or sexual violence

—Domestic Abuse Intervention Project, Duluth, Minnesota

DEEPENING

Mennonite therapist D. Pauline Zimmerman, in her book *If I Cry, Will Someone Understand Me?* writes on the importance of churches being educated on domestic violence, so that healing and hope may happen. Why does violence happen, even in Christian homes? I agree with many scholars that violence is a learned behavior. Dysfunctional families that tolerate violence produce children who abuse others as adults.

Kin-dom living is not about abusing—taking away dignity—but giving life and returning dignity.

Violence is about using force—physical, verbal, sexual, or spiritual. We often confuse conflict with violence. As humans, we experience conflict with other people who strongly disagree with us, with family members who offend us in some way, with the school system for not accepting a particular policy. Conflict is normal, but when we choose to resolve the conflict using violence, there is a problem.

Our Christian obligation is to denounce injustice. But churches on many occasions have protected the offender and accused the victim. In the name of the cross, Christians have committed violence. The vulnerable ones in society—women, the elderly, and children—have been victimized, those whom the Gospel calls "these little ones who believe in me" (Matthew 18:6). The individual and social temptation is to dominate the little ones and the most vulnerable. In the kin-dom of God we are called to speak up, to bring justice to these victims. Kin-dom living is not about abusing—taking away dignity—but giving life and returning dignity.

We can study and analyze violence to better understand it, but we cannot justify it. When we normalize violence, we keep it going. Violence is not a natural human tendency; it is a learned behavior. It can become so embedded in a person's way of living that it can be difficult to unlearn. The clue for transformation is to understand that the roots of family violence are attitudes that perpetuate control and abuse of power, the superiority of men over women and adults over children.

INTEGRATING

1. How can women recognize when excessive control is being exerted over them?

2. Share your struggles in knowing how to be helpful, while respecting boundaries, when concerned for another's safety.

3. The World Health Organization in their 2002 report noted that violence is both "predictable and preventable." *Action:* As families of peace, we can work on prevention, making our homes a safe place.

CLOSING

Sing together: "Confitemini Domino (Come and fill our hearts), #59 in *Sing the Journey*

Pray: Read the words from *Sing the Story*, #192, or pray the following prayer.

God of peace, let us recognize and name the violence we see in our personal relationships. Help us to work to end violence in all its forms. Amen.

ten . . . .

Jesus as Our Model for Peacemaking

READING: Matthew 5:38-48

OVERVIEW

In these verses, a core biblical text for historic peace churches, Jesus does away with the old law of retaliation found in the Old Testament. Instead, he stops the cycle of violence, calling listeners to overcome the temptation to pay back.

Listening in the crowd are slaves, women, the poor, and others subject to dehumanizing treatment by those in power. Yet Jesus says, "If anyone strikes you on the right cheek, turn the other cheek." In that time, slave owners had the right to strike a disobedient slave. It was a punishment from a person of power to one of inferior status. But a strike twice from the master was considered a shameful, abusive act. Perhaps Jesus was suggesting a response that would expose the cruel treatment of those abusing their power.

Jesus' teachings tell us to resist evil. Breaking the cycle of violence includes exposing and denouncing the abuse, sharing the story with those who can help stop the violence. Jesus gives a new way of responding—to do no evil, but to speak up.

VISUAL: Tablecloth, broken and mended pot

GATHERING

Martin Luther King Jr. once said in a sermon, "If we continue to practice the eye-for-an-eye law, finally we will all end up blind." Christians have a higher law, the law of love—not the law of payback.

"My anger blinds me; I get out of control and hurt people with my words and actions." I have heard this confession over and over in my practice. In becoming families of peace, we need to be clear that we mean the peace of Jesus. The biblical definition of peace is found in the word *Shalom*, well-being in a holistic sense. This is God's desire for us. Jesus, in his humanity, lived out the model of peacemaking everywhere he went. His miracles, liberating from demons, feeding the people, and teachings exemplified how to live that peace.

Think of two examples in Jesus' minstry when he confronted violence directly or indirectly. Jesus worked with situations of injustice, mistreatment, and abuse. What was his method of confronting these evils?

DEEPENING

A key theme in the book of Matthew is *basileia,* the kin-dom of God. The actions that Jesus demonstrated showed that in the kin-dom of God there is no allowance for any kind of abusive actions. The early Anabaptists interpreted these texts as part of the "rule of love"—a call to love one's enemy rather than to seek revenge.

To denounce violence is an act of justice. Christians believe that Jesus' teachings should govern our relationships in society, both inside and outside family life. To resist evil should not mean avoiding conflict, but preventing violence. In doing this, we are giving peace a chance in our family life.

Living out kin-dom values starts at home, within family relationships. Nonviolence is a lifestyle that aims to eliminate violence, denounce injustices, and find peaceful ways of resolving conflict. A commitment to nonviolence requires a spirituality of seeing the other with dignity, equality, and God's redeeming love.

A commitment to nonviolence requires a spirituality of seeing the other with dignity, equality, and God's redeeming love.

Jesus wants to live not only in our hearts, but in our families. Many of Jesus' miracles and signs took place in domestic situations, intended to restore or heal family members. Jesus wants to reign in the homes of those who serve him. The best step toward transforming society is to make a commitment to nonviolence in the home.

INTEGRATING

1. Reflect on times when you have experienced anger in your family. How can anger be handled in a positive way to build up the family?

2. How do you validate your own anger while still treating another person as worthy of respect?

3. Even if physical violence is not present, how can anger be destructive or hurtful to others?

4. How do we speak the truth in love?

CLOSING

Sing together: "Make me a channel of your peace," #56 in *Sing the Journey*.

Pray: God, *make us vessels of peace who can use anger positively to build up others and create more peaceful families. Forgive us for the times we are angry and do not follow the model of Jesus' positive anger. Amen.*

eleven . . . .

The Family of God

READING: Mark 3:31-35

OVERVIEW

Imagine you are the mother or sister of Jesus as you hear these strong words from his mouth: "Who are my mother and brothers?" How would it feel to stand in the door of the house, with other people listening, as Jesus ignores your request to see him?

This text follows the earlier statement in verse 19b, "Then he went home . . ." Jesus has completed calling out the twelve disciples, performed several miracles, and taught around the region. Now he is in his hometown. His family is trying to be with him, to protect him from the accusations and name-calling he is already receiving. It has to be painful for Mary to hear people linking her son with Satan. Jesus' family is acting out of love. They arrive at the house as Jesus is teaching, and it sounds as if they are interrupting Jesus' mission. Still, we are curious. What did Jesus really mean when he said, looking at the people around him, "Here are my mother and my brothers!" (v. 34).

VISUAL: Tablecloth, basket of fruit, church directory or photos of different people in your church/group

GATHERING

My husband tells proudly how his parents in Pigeon, Michigan, raised more than 20 foster children when he was growing up (not all at the same time!). Mother Albrecht and her wonderful family shared Jesus' love to these children. Their small mission church welcomed the children as well, giving them a large family to visit every Sunday—the church.

An older couple recently shared how they adopted three "great-grandchildren," children of a young, single mother in their community, and how much this means to them. They have been estranged from one of their own children for many years, with all efforts at healing the rifts rejected. At Christmas, their adopted great-granddaughter gave them a little wall hanging with the words, " Some families are made in the heart."

DEEPENING

Jesus formed a new family from his followers. Why did he seem to reject his biological family? Did he feel they limited his mission? Sometimes it is hard for parents to let go of growing-up children. I can hear my daughters telling me, "Mami, let me go!" We fear for their safety. We don't want to see them get hurt.

Many have observed how the practices of early Christians and even Jesus' words reflect an almost "anti-family" feeling. For example, the gospels refer to leaving family behind, not attending to duties in being a father, etc. This could have been a criticism of the forms of family in Jesus' time. Many of his followers were being rejected by their families, so they found a new family among the community of believers.

What does it mean to be God's family? God's family should reflect healthy relationships. Colossians 3:12 and 15 (NIV) say, "Therefore, as God's chosen people, holy, and dearly beloved, clothe yourselves with compassion, kindness, humility, gentleness and patience . . . Let the peace of Christ rule in your hearts, since as members of one body you were called to peace." These are attitudes that characterize relationships among Christian believers. When our life offers

In the Mark text, Jesus defines the new alternative family: "Whoever does the will of God is my brother and sister and mother."

these fruits, we are instilling kin-dom values in another person's life. Like a mustard seed, that love will spread. But this is possible only when our families have peace.

How does the church promote good, healthy families? Do we have a clear image of what that looks like? In the Mark text, Jesus defines the new alternative family: "Whoever does the will of God is my brother and sister and mother" (v. 35). The commitment toward transformation starts by paying attention to God's will.

A church is not just four walls. It is the body of Christ and the family of God. The church is made up of smaller units, families and individuals, living in different neighborhoods and contributing toward a culture of peace. As Jesus indicates in Mark, the biological ties do not matter as much as being part of those who bear fruit in obedience to God.

INTEGRATING

1 . If you are in a church family, how is it a place of refuge and spiritual connection for you?

2 . In what ways do you wish your church family would be more of a place of refuge? Can you think of ways to help it be more so?

3. Share stories of how church groups have welcomed others who are very different from them.

4. How does your church family provide an example of what peace in the family is about?

5. In a culture that places high priority on the nuclear family, are there ways we should limit our commitments to our nuclear family so we can be more faithful to our church family?

CLOSING

Sing together: "Help us to help each other," #362 in *Hymnal: A Worship Book.*

Pray: *Sheltering God, help us to make the church a place of refuge for those who are in need. Give us wisdom to build peace as we welcome those who are different from ourselves. Amen.*

twelve . . . .

Toward a Culture of Peace

READING: Luke 4:16-21

OVERVIEW

Luke 4 begins at the start of Jesus' ministry, following his temptation in the wilderness. In verses 16-21, Jesus is reading the Scripture in his home synagogue in Nazareth. He selects from the scroll of Isaiah a portion of the songs of "the Servant of the Lord" (Isaiah 61:1-2 and 58:6), using these ancient writings to confirm his calling and vision of the kin-dom. The words are familiar to the people of his hometown, but Jesus puts a new twist on the words, telling them, "Today this Scripture has been fulfilled."

The Isaiah text Jesus reads sets out the values of God's kin-dom in building a culture of peace:

- To bring good news to the poor
- To proclaim release to the captives
- To restore sight to the blind
- To let the oppressed go free
- To proclaim the year of the Lord's favor

VISUAL: Tablecloth, scroll (or Bible open to Isaiah 61), lighted candle

GATHERING

"Peace at any price." Those were my friend Maria's words when she heard her children arguing with each other. I asked, "What do you mean, Maria?" In a fearful voice, she confessed that she gets anxious when she hears her children raising their voices, yelling at each other. As a pastor, I understand where that fear comes from. She saw abuse when she was a child and wants peace in her home.

I invited Maria to examine with me how Jesus brought peace. In Jesus' time, the Roman Empire's political peace was known as *Pax Romana*. The empire used force to bring "peace," but Jesus' peace came not through violence, but through loving one's enemies.

In this last session on becoming families of peace, we return to Jesus' mission. Read the song of Mary, known as the *Magnificat*, in Luke 1:46-55. What kind of family environment did Mary and Joseph provide for Jesus and his siblings? This song expresses Mary's feelings when she was chosen to carry the "Good News" into this world. She felt empowered with the privilege given to her. Jesus' surroundings shaped his sensitivity toward those in need. From humble descent, he came to teach us the gospel of peace.

DEEPENING

In the same way Jesus did, we must speak and live out the good news of the kin-dom within our homes. We need to feel that the Spirit of God is among us to proclaim healing, restoration, and peace in our families.

Families today face unique challenges; instant messaging does not mean we are having good communication. That everyone in the family has a cell phone does not translate into being connected. Sometimes these high-tech devices are just one more reason to avoid having human, skin-to-skin contact with children. We are allowing these text messages to substitute for a hug or a kiss. People need human contact in order to build a culture of peace. Electronic devices are useful in maintaining the connections we already have; unfortunately they are often used to avoid or substitute for the real connections we all need. *Cybernetic* families are just not the same as *energetic* families fired up with Jesus' love and peace.

Electronic devices are useful in maintaining the connections we already have; unfortunately they are often used to avoid or substitute for the real connections we all need.

The five indicators of God's kin-dom we read in Luke 4:18-19 can bring healing and hope for families, releasing those members who are held captive to abuse in non-healthy family systems. In healthy families, we will find that freedom reigns, with structure and order. In homes with harmony, we celebrate with each member their milestones, their rights of passage as they move on to next stages in life. Translate into your family life how these five elements will look.

Just as the Holy Spirit empowered Jesus to accomplish his mission on earth, today we can count on that same power to bring these changes home. Theologian Jack Suderman reminds us that our God is a God of peace, harmony, holistic well-being, and reconciliation among humans. These characteristics of the kin-dom of God should be visible in our lives. How is your family exhibiting the culture of peace today? Start at home!

Clues for transformation will be found wherever we see the mission of Jesus accomplished. It is easy to serve others we may not know; the challenge is to serve within the family.

When these actions are done as a manifestation of love, we are contributing toward change—first in our homes, and second in a world that needs transformation.

INTEGRATING

1 . How are technological relationships different from face-to-face relationships?

2 . How can speaking for peace bring conflict or make people uncomfortable?

3 . Reflect on your own gifts and calling and write a personal mission statement. How do these gifts complement your commitments within your home and church families?

4 . With your family members, reflect on your mission and compose together a peace mission statement. For an example, see pages 66-67.

CLOSING

Sing together: "If you believe and I believe," #32 in *Sing the Journey*.

Pray: *God, be for us the model of peace. Help us to make our families models of peace for a violent and hurting world. Help us to bring healing and restoration in the family of God. Amen.*

t h i r t e e n . . . .

Celebrating Being Families of Peace

VISUAL FOCUS

Display the symbols from all the previous sessions in the center of a table covered with a colorful tablecloth. Include a lighted pillar candle. Sit around the table.

GATHERING

Leader: Let us worship together and offer thanksgiving to God for all the blessings we have received by God's grace and mercy. We celebrate together our families. As we are around the table we remember all the miracles Jesus did in homes—healing, forgiving, saving, teaching, and eating with people he cared for, even his enemies. Now, let us come with a worshipful spirit, allowing the Spirit of God to move among us.

Opening Prayer:

    Leader: Most holy God,
          the source of all good desires,
          all right judgments,
          and all just works:

    Group: **Give to us, your servants,**
          that peace which the world cannot give,
          so that our minds may be fixed on the
          doing of your will,

and that we, being delivered from the fear
   of all enemies,
may live in peace and quietness;
through the mercies of Christ Jesus, our
   Savior. Amen.

—Hymnal: A Worship Book #742

Song: Hymnal: A Worship Book #1, "What is this place?"

LITURGY FOR THE FAMILY*

Leader: Blessed are the people who do not walk in the counsel of the wicked.

Women on left: But their delight is in the law of the LORD, and on God's law they meditate day and night.

Women on right: They are like a tree planted by streams of water, which yields its fruit in season and whose leaf does not wither.

All: We are here to celebrate families moving toward shalom. By God's grace, we want to declare that peace is possible.

Older women: Joseph's brothers sold him to slavery in Egypt, then went there for grain. Joseph cried out to them, "I am Joseph! Is my father still living?"

Younger women: His brothers couldn't answer him, because they were terrified at his presence.

Older women: So Joseph said to them, "Come close to me." He threw his arms around his brother Benjamin and wept, and Benjamin hugged him, weeping. Joseph kissed them all and wept over them. Then his brothers could talk with him.

....
* Liturgy developed by Pastor Janet Brenneman, Laurel Street
Mennonite Church, Lancaster, Pa., for a series on Family and Shalom.

Leader: All of you, live in harmony; be sympathetic, love each other as brothers and sisters, be compassionate and humble.

Women on left: Naomi in grief and anger returned to Bethlehem. "Do not call me Naomi. Call me Mara, because the Almighty has made my life very bitter. I went away full, but the Lord has brought me back empty."

Leader: Go ahead and be angry. You do well to be angry— but don't use your anger as fuel for revenge. And don't stay angry. Do not go to bed angry.

Women on right: Jesus' mother and brothers came to see him. A crowd told him, "Your mother and brothers are outside looking for you."

Younger women: "Who are my mother and my brothers?" he asked.

Older women: He looked at those seated in a circle around him and said, "Whoever does God's will is my brother and sister and mother."

All: Let love be genuine; hate what is evil, hold fast to what is good; love one another with mutual affection; outdo one another in showing honor. Serve the Lord. Rejoice in hope!

Scriptures, adapted: Psalm 1:1, 3; Genesis 45:3-4, 14-15; 1 Peter 3:8; Ruth 1:19-21; Ephesians 4:26-27; Mark 3:31-35; Romans 12:9-12

REFLECTION

Song: *Hymnal: A Worship Book* #545, "Be thou my vision"

Read and reflect:
Several stories in the Bible tell of women who conceive a child after much prayer, and then turn around to "give them

up." Hannah gives Samuel to service in the temple. Ruth gives her firstborn, Obed, to the widow Naomi. And Mary, knowing the child she births will belong to God, still agrees to bring Jesus into this world.

I am moved by the offerings of these women. They detached themselves from children that were rightfully theirs. As mothers soon learn to understand, a child is born to them to raise and eventually let go into a world that may not appreciate that sacrificial gift. Fortunately, as women we give birth in many other ways—in ideas for a committee, a creative piece of art, organizing to help the needy, doing volunteer work, or babysitting children that are hurting. Teaching and preaching are also ways we birth new creation through the Word, into a world that needs God's peace.

Around the table share: What impact have these Bible studies had on your personal life? What new ideas did you conceive in this journey together? When you examine your family's actions, values, and interactions in light of the Scriptures in this study, how do they measure up?

Take time to pray for one another, bless each other, and rejoice that together as women of God we will contribute toward the kin-dom of God here on earth, proclaiming "Peace on earth and good will to all" (Luke 2:14).

CLOSING

Prayer: Read together the following words adapted from the prayer of St. Francis of Assisi.

> **Lord, make me an instrument of your peace.**
> **Where there is hate, may I bring love;**
> **Where there is anger, let us learn to forgive**
> **And heal our wounds;**

Where there is darkness, to understand,
in order to look for nonviolent solutions together;
Where there are differences, to know how to mediate,
to listen to the position of the other person,
in order to grow as a person;
Where there is sadness, to understand the reasons for
these feelings,
And to learn to express myself better, in order to
achieve true happiness.

O Divine Master, help me not to seek that my position
always wins,
But that we all win in my home.
Help me to express my love with words and tender
gestures toward my family.

Help us to build peace in our families,
So that in this way we can be instruments of peace
in our world. Amen.

Songs: *Sing the Journey* #56, "Make me a channel of your peace"
Sing the Story #16, "Peace before us"

Appendix

The Seven Manifestations of a Healthy and Peaceful Family

1 . Create change. Romans 12:2 motivates us to be transformed by the renewing of our mind in order to discern the will of God that is good, acceptable, and perfect. We create change when we live up to God's calling, starting at home.

2 . Be a blessing. Our mission as families is to be a blessing to others, just as God told Abraham he would be a blessing (Genesis 12:3b). To be a blessing means to be a role model.

3 . Put family first. In order to have families that are together/unified, we need to work at it. We need to nurture our families with "family time" every day. We need a regular bonding time, both one-on-one and as a complete unit.

4 . Think win-win. Learn how to negotiate so that all members of the family "win"—feel heard and respected. Mark 10:43 says, "Whoever wishes to become great among you must be your servant."

5 . Learn to listen and understand. The art of communication is mastered first by active listening and understanding the other's feelings and thoughts. This builds relationships of trust and love. Ephesians 5:21 and 6:4: "Be subject to one another" and "Do not provoke your children to anger."

6 . Have healthy interdependence. The whole, which is the family, becomes greater than the sum of the parts. The family is where the fruits of the Spirit should be present: "love, joy, peace, patience, kindness, generosity, faithfulness, gentleness, and self-control" (Galatians 5:22-23).

7. Love one another. First Corinthians 13:13 begins by stating, "the greatest of these is love." This is not simply describing a physical, romantic love—not even a feeling, but the commitment to love the other, to be there for one another. It is God's perfect *agape* love, not the *filio o eros*, that will keep the family together.

—*Adapted by Elizabeth Soto Albrecht from* The 7 Habits of Highly Effective Families *by Stephen R. Covey (New York: St. Martins Griffin, 1997). Biblical references added.*

Example of a Family Mission Statement
by Frank, Elizabeth, Yentli, and Sara, April 2003

In our family we want to serve God through the humanity that surrounds us. We will treat each other with respect and tolerance. We want to act with God's love between ourselves, and being filled with joy and security we will share this love with other families in our church and community.

We will seek justice and peace between ourselves and will also share this gift with others. We want to find equilibrium between sharing our time amoung ourselves and with others.

We believe that good communication is basic in our family, and we want to dialogue peacefully. We want to work through our differences in calmness, and when we make a mistake both ask for forgiveness and be forgiving. When a child commits an error he/she still has the right to express him/herself respectfully.

We want to be a family that shares the daily chores of the house and do so with happiness.

It is important to our family that we be pro-active and think before we act. When something we are doing in the family is not working, we will reflect together about the change we want to make.

We want to serve the Lord, contributing to society!

About Mennonite Women Canada

"A Place to Belong"

Motto

As each has received a gift, employ it for one another, as good stewards of God's varied grace. 1 Peter 4:10

Mission Statement

Mennonite Women Canada (MW Canada) encourages women to be personally reconciled and committed to Christ and seeks to call forth the variety of gifts given by the Holy Spirit to build the church of Jesus Christ.

We commit ourselves to:

- Promote spiritual growth through Bible study, prayer, other Christian disciplines and fellowship
- Discern and nurture women's gifts and skills for leadership and service in the local church, the community and the world
- Build relationships and networks for support, affirmation, discernment, witness, service and celebration
- Support and strengthen the mission outreach of **Mennonite Church Canada**.

We do this through:

- Annual meeting and workshop at Mennonite Church Canada Assembly

- Inter-provincial/regional organizations

- Newsletters

- Scholarships for theological study through **Spiritual Growth Assistance Fund**

- Financial help for Canadian Mennonite University students participating in a practicum through the **Service and Internship Program**

- **Pennies & Prayer Inheritance Fund** (PPIF), a home for gifts made in honour/memory of loved ones

- Supporting women working in Mennonite Church Canada's ministries with funds from the PPIF

- Stories of **"Women Walking Together in Faith"** in *Canadian Mennonite*

- Publishing an annual Anabaptist Bible study guide with Mennonite Women USA

- A blogspot: www.mennowomencanada.blogspot.com

We as Mennonite Women Canada are striving to do God's will and work where we are to the best of our ability. You too can be a part!

For more information, visit the Mennonite Women Canada website at www.mennonitechurch.ca/mwc/.

Or write to:
Mennonite Women Canada
c/o Mennonite Church Canada
600 Shaftesbury Blvd.
Winnipeg, MB R3P 0M4

About Mennonite Women USA

Jesus said: "I am the vine. You are the branches." John 15:5

Mission Statement

Our mission at Mennonite Women USA is to empower women and women's groups as we nurture our life in Christ through studying the Bible, using our gifts, hearing each other, and engaging in mission and service.

In living our mission, Mennonite Women USA:

- Provides **Sister Care** seminars for effective lay caring in the congregation.

- Shares stories of women of all ages and backgrounds in *timbrel*, a magazine published six times a year. *Timbrel* helps women be in conversation together with God on a variety of themes: growing in our personal relationship with Christ, sharing God's healing and hope in our families, churches and communities and connecting women with resources.

- Funds scholarships for women worldwide for church leadership training through our **International Women's Fund**.

- Co-sponsors biennial **Women in Conversation retreats** in the East and the Midwest—a time for spiritual nourishment, reflection with God and warm fellowship with other women.

- Connects and provides resources for **women's groups** throughout Mennonite Church USA. An Anabaptist Bible study guide is produced annually. Sister Care seminars provide tools for effective lay caring in the congregation.

- Fosters relationships around the world through the **Sister-Link** program—emphasizing mutual giving and receiving and validating a wide variety of gifts. Sister-Links connect women globally and locally through prayer, letter writing, sharing resources, and face-to-face visits.

Vision Statement

Mennonite Women USA invites women across generations, cultures, and places to share and honor our stories, care for each other, and express our prophetic voice boldly as we seek to follow Christ.

We'd love to tell you more about our ministry.

Learn more about Mennonite Women USA programs—and get a little lift in your day—by signing up for our free monthly e-letter, "A Postcard and a Prayer." Just send your name, address, and email to office@MennoniteWomenUSA.org.

You may also access our website for our latest news and stories: www.MennoniteWomenUSA.org.

Mennonite Women USA
722 Main Street
Newton, KS 6714-0347
(316) 283-4396
office@MennoniteWomenUSA.org

About the Writer

E lizabeth Soto Albrecht is the author of *Family Violence: Reclaiming a Theology of Nonviolence* (2008). The book received a 2009 award from the Catholic Press Association in the category of Gender Issues as a book that "challenges Christian communities of all traditions to preach and practice nonviolence as a core principle of Jesus' ministry."

Born in Puerto Rico, Elizabeth spent some of her growing-up years in Chicago. She now lives in Lancaster, Pennsylvania, with her husband Frank and two teenage daughters, Yentli and Sara. The family served in Colombia, South America, with Mennonite Central Committee for seven years. During that time Elizabeth was ordained for ministry in the Colombian Mennonite Church and pastored a congregation. The family is currently actively involved with Laurel Street Mennonite Church, Lancaster.

Elizabeth is a member of the Executive Board of Mennonite Church USA and participated in Mennonite Women USA's spring 2009 strategic envisioning. She works at Lancaster Theological Seminary as coordinator of field education and consultant for their cross-cultural seminar trips. She also serves as associate chaplain at Women & Babies Hospital of Lancaster.

Elizabeth enjoys taking walks around the neighborhood with her husband or friends "who want to be more healthy" and reading novels by "good Latina writers." She also likes to celebrate Fridays with her daughters, taking them out for a movie, ice-cream, or Chinese or Puerto Rican food.